Wonders of the
Natural World

TJ Rob

Wonders of the Natural World
By TJ Rob
Wonders of the World — Volume 1

Copyright Text TJ Rob, 2016

All rights reserved. No part of the book may be reproduced in any form without permission in writing from the author. Reviewers may quote brief passages in review.
ISBN 978-1-988695-21-1

Disclaimer:
No part of this book may be reproduced in any form or by any means, mechanical or electronic, including photocopying or recording, or by an information storage and retrieval system, or transmitted by email without permission in writing from the publisher. This book is for entertainment purposes only. The views expressed are those of author alone.

Published by:
TJ Rob
Suite 609

440-10816 Macleod Trail SE
Calgary, AB T2J 5N8 www.TJRob.com

Photo Credits: Images used under license from Shutterstock.com, Flickr.com, Pixabay.com, Creative Commons and Public Domain:

Cover page, Gunnar Hildonen /Flickr.com; Cover page, Mariamichelle/Pixabay.com; Cover page, ELI Duke/ Flickr.com; Cover page, Sahajesh Patel /Flickr.com; Cover page, Apollomelos~commonswiki /Public Domain; Back Page, miquitos/Flickr.com; pg. 1, Mark Lewinski /Flickr.com; pg. 1, Andreas Karbanis /Flickr.com; pg. 4, Rdevany CC BY-SA 3.0/Creative Commons; pg. 4, By Mmikle CC BY-SA 4.0-3.0-2.5-2.0-1.0/Creative Commons; pg. 5, Public Domain/Pixabay.com; pg. 5, By Jamling Tenzing Norgay CC BY-SA 3.0/Creative Commons; pg. 5, By Igomezc CC BY-SA 3.0/Creative Commons; pg. 6, By I Kmusser CC BY 2.5/Creative Commons; pg. 7, Public Domain /Wikimedia Commons; pg. 7, Mike Lee/Flickr.com; pg. 7, By Z22 CC BY-SA 4.0 /Wikimedia Commons; pg. 8, kavram/Shutterstock.com; pg. 9, irisphoto1/Shutterstock.com; pg. 9, Rob Swanson/Shutterstock.com; pg. 9, Israel_photo_gallery /Flickr.com; pg. 10, Daniel Schwen CC BY-SA 4.0, /Wikimedia Commons; pg. 11, Beatrice Murch /Flickr.com; pg. 12, RMehra~commonswiki CC BY-SA 3.0, /Wikimedia Commons; pg. 12, Public Domain/Pixabay.com; pg. 13, By PP Yoonus/Public Domain; pg. 13, By McKay SavageCC BY 2.0 /Wikimedia Commons; pg. 14, By cobaltcigs CC BY-SA 3.0 /Wikimedia Commons; pg. 14, By ESO/B. Tafreshi CC BY 4.0/ Wikimedia Commons; pg. 15, D'July/Shutterstock.com; pg. 15, gary yim/Shutterstock.com; pg. 17, Venezolana orgullosa CC BY-SA 3.0 /Wikimedia Commons; pg. 18, Neal Parish CC BY-SA 2.0/Wikimedia Commons; pg. 19, Jim Bahn CC BY 2.0/Wikimedia Commons; pg. 20, Alewtincka/Shutterstock.com; pg. 21, Kmusser CC BY-SA 3.0/Wikimedia Commons; pg. 21, A C Moraes /Flickr.com; pg. 22, Ninara/Flickr.com; pg. 23, arazu/ Shutterstock.com; pg. 24, NSF/Josh Landis/Public Domain; pg. 25, NASA/Public Domain; pg. 25, Public Domain/Wikimedia Commons; pg. 26, Gunnar Hildonen/Flickr.com; pg. 27, Greg Clarke/Flickr.com; pg. 28, By Pfly - NASA/Public Domain.com; pg. 28, Dr. Morley Read/Shutterstock.com; pg. 29, Dr. Morley Read/ Shutterstock.com; pg. 30, Sergey Gabdurakhmanov/Flickr.com; pg. 31, Day Donaldson /Flickr.com; pg. 31, Pavelblazek CC BY-SA 3.0 /Wikimedia Commons; pg. 31, Per Harald Olsen CC BY-SA 3.0/Wikimedia Commons; pg. 31, Sansculotte on de.wikipedia CC BY-SA 3.0/Wikimedia Commons

TABLE OF CONTENTS

	Page
The Highest Mountain	4
The Deepest Part of the Ocean	6
The Lowest Point on Earth	8
The Biggest Cave System on Earth	10
The Wettest Place on Earth	12
The Driest Place on Earth	14
The Highest Waterfall	16
The Tallest Tree on Earth	18
The Biggest River on Earth	20
The Hottest Place on Earth	22
The Coldest Place on Earth	24
The Most Spectacular Light Show	26
The Biggest Rainforest	28
The Deepest and Oldest Lake on Earth	30
Please leave a review and Other EXCITING books by TJ Rob	32

The Highest Mountain
MOUNT EVEREST

Mount Everest is Earth's highest mountain. Its peak is 29,028 feet (8,848 meters) above sea level. That is 5 and a half miles (8.85 km) high, or the equivalent of the size of almost 20 Empire State Buildings stacked on top of one another.

Everest is found in part of the Himalaya mountain range. It is on the border of Nepal and Tibet. Tibet, India, and Nepal are all visible from the top.

Everest was first climbed in 1953 by Edmund Hillary and Tenzing Norgay.

Since then about 4,000 people have tried to climb Everest.

Only 660 have succeeded. 142 people have died trying.

Hillary and Tenzing

Deepest Part of the Ocean
MARIANA TRENCH

The Mariana Trench or Marianas Trench is the deepest part of the world's oceans.

It is located in the Western Pacific Ocean.

The trench is about 1,580 miles (2,550 km) long but has an average width of only 43 miles (69 km).

It reaches a maximum known depth of 36,070 feet (10,994 m) at a small valley in its floor known as the Challenger Deep. It is so deep that it could swallow Mount Everest with plenty of room to spare!

At the bottom of the trench the water pressure is the equivalent of having 50 jumbo jets piled on top of a person.

The temperature at the bottom is 33.8° to 39.2° Fahrenheit (1° to 4° Celsius).

Only 3 people have ever been to the bottom of the Challenger Deep, in specially designed diving submersibles.

Compare that to 12 people that have landed on the Moon.

1960 — TRIESTE

2 pilots - Jacques Piccard and Don Walsh

Descent: 4 hours, 48 minutes

20 minutes at the bottom

2012 — DEEPSEA CHALLENGER

1 pilot – James Cameron

Descent: 2 hours, 30 minutes

3 hours at the bottom

Lowest Point on Earth
THE DEAD SEA

The Dead Sea is a salt lake bordered by Jordan to the east and Israel and the West Bank to the west.

Its surface and shores are 1,407 feet (429 meters) below sea level, Earth's lowest elevation on land. The Dead Sea is 997 feet (304 m) deep.

It is also one of the world's saltiest bodies of water. It is 9.6 times as salty as the ocean. Animals and fish cannot survive in the Dead Sea, hence its name. Only tiny quantities of bacteria and fungi have been found in the Dead Sea.

Because it is so salty the water of the Dead Sea is very dense. This makes swimming very difficult. You can only float on the surface.

The Dead Sea is 31 miles (50 km) long and 9 miles (15 km) wide at its widest point.

The Dead Sea has attracted visitors from around the Mediterranean for thousands of years. It was one of the world's first health resorts.

The salt has been used in many different products — from Egyptian mummification to fertilizers. People also use the salt and the minerals from the Dead Sea to create cosmetics and skin care products.

The Biggest Cave System on Earth
MAMMOTH CAVES

Mammoth Cave is the longest cave system known in the world. It has over 400 miles (640 km) of surveyed passageways. It is located in Kentucky, USA.

The Mammoth Cave system is by far the world's longest known cave system, being over twice as long as the second-longest cave system in Mexico.

The caves were first discovered by Native Americans about 4,000 years ago, who used them for over 2,000 years.

Today 400,000 visitors are guided through the cave system each year.

Over 130 different animal species can be found in the caves and the river system that flows through the cave. Some animals are visitors and others use Mammoth Cave as their home.

Cave shrimp, bats, beetles, fish, raccoons and bullfrogs are a few animals found in Mammoth Caves.

The Wettest Place on Earth
MEGHALAYA STATE, INDIA

Meghalaya is a state in North-East India. The name means "the land of the clouds" in Sanskrit.

2 villages in Meghalaya State hold records for being the wettest places on Earth.

The village of Cherrapunjee holds the record for the most rainfall in only 2 days — 98 inches (2.49 meters) from the 15th to the 16th June 1995.

This would be enough water to cover the head of the tallest basketball player on Earth with room to spare.

According to the Guinness Book of World Records, the village of Mawsynram received 1,000 inches or 83 feet (26 meters) of rainfall in 1985. This is a record for the most rain in a single year.

With an annual rainfall of more than 468 inches or 39 feet (11.88 meters), this gives Mawsynram the title of "wettest place on Earth."

This means that every year in Mawsynram it rains enough to completely cover the top of the goal posts on a NFL football field!

The Driest Place on Earth

South America

THE ATACAMA DESERT, SOUTH AMERICA

The Atacama Desert is a plateau in South America, covering a 600 mile (1,000 km) strip of land on the Pacific coast, West of the Andes mountains. It is the driest non-polar desert in the world. It covers parts of Chile, Peru, Bolivia and Argentina

The average rainfall is about 0.6 inches (15 mm) per year, although some weather stations in the Atacama have never received rain.

Scientists believe that the Atacama may not have had any rainfall from 1570 to 1971, a period of over 400 years!

The Atacama Desert has been too dry to support vegetation for at least 3 million years. This makes the Atacama the oldest dry region on earth.

In some parts of the Atacama the soil has been compared to that of Mars. NASA uses the Atacama Desert to test equipment for future missions to Mars.

The Highest Waterfall
ANGEL FALLS, VENEZUELA

Angel Falls in Venezuela is the world's highest uninterrupted waterfall.

It has a height of 3,212 feet high (979 meters) and a plunge of 2,648 feet (807 meters).

Angel Falls is about 20 times higher than Niagara Falls.

The waterfall drops over the edge of the Auyantepui Mountain.

Angel Falls is 492 feet (150 meters) wide at its base.

A visitor can feel small drops of water spray at a distance of 1 mile (1.6 km) away.

Angel Falls is named after an American pilot, Jimmie Angel, who had airplane trouble and landed on a nearby flat mountain top close to the falls in 1937.

Along with his wife and two other people, it took them 11 days to climb down the mountain in the middle of the South American wilderness.

The Tallest Tree on Earth
GENERAL SHERMAN, Giant Sequoia

General Sherman is a Giant Sequoia tree located in the Giant Forest of Sequoia National Park in California, USA.

(18) It is the largest known living single stem tree on Earth.

With a height of 275 feet (83.8 meters) and a diameter of 25 feet (7.7 meters), the General Sherman tree is among the tallest and widest of all trees on the planet.

It also has an estimated age of 2,300 – 2,700 years old, making this tree one of the longest-lived of all trees on the planet.

The tree was named after the American Civil War general William Tecumseh Sherman in 1879.

The Biggest River on Earth
THE AMAZON RIVER

The Amazon River is the biggest river in the world, measured by the amount of water that flows down it.

The Amazon River is located in South America. It runs through 7 countries — Guyana, Ecuador, Venezuela, Bolivia, Brazil, Colombia and Peru.

On average 31 million (31,700,646) US Gallons (120 million liters) of water flows out of its mouth into the Atlantic Ocean every second.

This is the equivalent of completely emptying about 20 Olympic sized swimming pools every second!

The Amazon River is approximately 4,000 miles (6400 km) long, and reaches over 120 miles (190km) wide at its mouth.

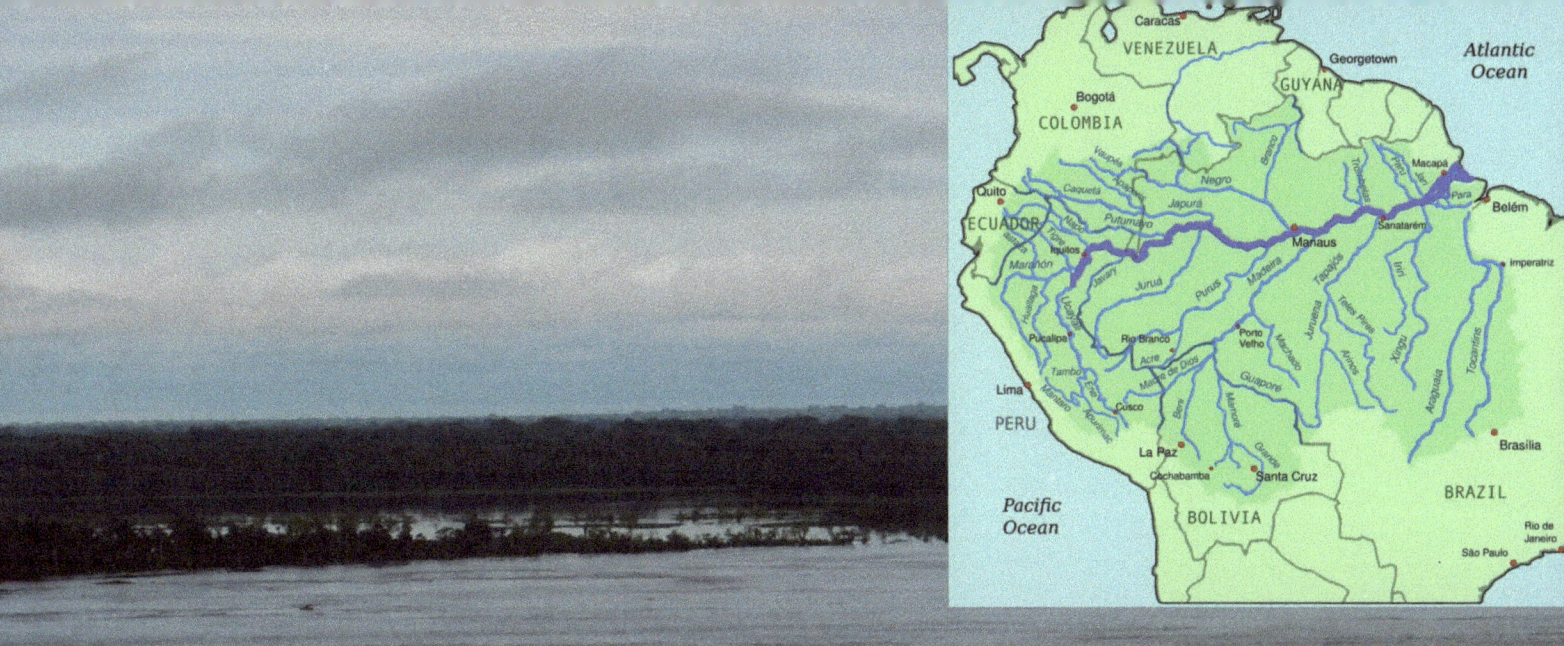

There are no bridges that cross the Amazon, because the majority of the Amazon River runs through rainforests rather than roads or cities.

There are over 3000 known species of fish that live in the Amazon River, with more being discovered all the time.

The Piranha, a meat eating type of fish, is found in the Amazon River. Piranhas are known to attack in groups, preying on animals that stray into the water.

Another animal that lives in the Amazon River is the Giant Anaconda, one of the largest snakes in the world. The Giant Anaconda lives in the shallow waters of the Amazon Basin. They will attack larger animals, such as goats, that get too close to the edge of the river.

The Hottest Place on Earth
LUT DESERT, IRAN

The Lut Desert in Iran is an area so isolated that no one is around to regularly monitor temperatures.

A NASA satellite was able to measure temperatures in the Lut Desert from space over a 7 year period.

> In 5 out of the 7 years — 2004, 2005, 2006, 2007 and 2009 — the hottest spot on Earth was found to be in the Lut Desert.

In 2005, a temperature of 159.3 degrees Fahrenheit (70.72 degrees Celsius) was measured in the Lut Desert. This is the highest reading ever officially recorded for any location on Earth.

That is hot enough to fry an egg! It is so hot in the Lut desert that not even germs and bacteria can survive.

Scientists have tested this by opening containers of sterilized milk and leaving them sitting in the sun in the Lut Desert. The milk did not spoil!

The Coldest Place on Earth
VOSTOK WEATHER STATION, ANTARCTICA

The Russian weather station, Vostok, is about 800 miles (1,300 km) from the South Pole, at the center of the East Antarctic Ice Sheet.

It is by far the coldest spot on earth. On July 21, 1983 the lowest temperature recorded on Earth was at Vostok. It was −128.6 °F (−89.2 °C). At this temperature you would get frostbite in less than 1 minute.

Vostok also recorded a windchill of −255°F (-124°C) on August 4, 2005.

Vostok Station was built in 1957 and is a permanent research station. The station is at 11,444 feet (3,488 meters) above sea level.

It is one of the most isolated research stations on the Antarctic Continent.

The station normally has 25 Scientists and Engineers in the Summer. In Winter, the number of people drops to 13.

They study the Earth's climate, magnetic field and levels of radiation from the Sun.

The Most Spectacular Light Show
THE NORTHERN LIGHTS OR AURORA BOREALIS

The Northern Lights or Aurora Borealis are a natural light display in the sky that is powered by the Solar Wind as it passes Earth.

After a magnetic storm on the Sun, a stream of particles called the Solar Wind, is released into the upper atmosphere of the Sun. The Solar Wind takes two days to reach the Earth and affect the Earth's atmosphere with increased Northern Lights.

Atoms in the Earth's upper atmosphere are struck by electrons and protons in the Solar Wind causing the bright colors.

The Northern Lights are viewed in the Northern Hemisphere. The Southern Lights can be viewed in the Southern Hemisphere and look similar to the Northern Lights. The official names are Aurora Borealis in the Northern Hemisphere and the Aurora Australis in the Southern Hemisphere.

The Aurora Borealis was named by Pierre Gassendi in 1621. Aurora is the Roman goddess of dawn. Borealis is the Greek word for the north wind.

The four best months to watch the Aurora Borealis are February, March, September and October.

The Northern Lights occur between 50 and 200 miles (80—320 km) above the Earth. They can last for a few hours. They fill the sky with green, pink, yellow and orange lights. Green is the most common color and red is the rarest.

Biggest Rain Forest
THE AMAZON RAINFOREST

Amazon Rainforest

The Amazon Rain Forest is the largest rain forest in the world. It is bigger than all the other rain forests of the world added together. It is spread across 8 countries — Brazil, Bolivia, Columbia, French Guyana, Surinam, Peru, Ecuador and Venezuela. It covers about 2.1 million square miles (5.5 million square kilometers).

About 20 percent of the earth's oxygen content is produced by the Amazon Rain Forest.

It gets its name from the world's largest river that flows through it, the Amazon River.

The Amazon rainforest has an estimated 390 billion individual trees.

The region is home to about 2.5 million insect species, 40,000 plant species, 2,200 fishes, 2,000 birds, 427 mammals, 428 amphibians and 378 reptile species.

One in five of all the bird species in the world live in the rainforests of the Amazon.

Deepest and Oldest Lake on Earth

LAKE BAIKAL

Lake Baikal is the largest freshwater lake by volume in the world. It contains roughly 20% of the world's unfrozen surface fresh water. Lake Baikal is located North of Mongolia in Russia.

With a maximum depth of 5,387 feet (1,642 meters), Lake Baikal is the world's deepest lake. It contains more water than all the North American Great Lakes combined.

Lake Baikal is thought to be the world's oldest lake — 25 million years old.

It is the 7th largest lake in the world by surface area. Its surface area is equivalent to that of the country of Belgium. Lake Baikal is 395 miles (636 km) long and 48 miles (78 km) at its widest.

Standing on clear ice.

Lake Baikal has the purest fresh water on the planet. It is also the most transparent of all freshwater lakes. In some areas of the lake you can see the bottom at a depth of 132 feet (40 meters)! Ice in many places on the lake is completely clear.

1455 animal and fish species live in and around Lake Baikal. 75% of these can only be found in the Lake Baikal region.

The only freshwater seals in the world are found in Lake Baikal. There are 27 species of fish found nowhere else.

Baikal Freshwater Seal

Baikal Omul

THANKS FOR READING!

Please leave a review at the website where you bought this book and tell others what you liked about it.

Visit www.TJRob.com for a FREE eBook and to see TJ Rob's other exciting books

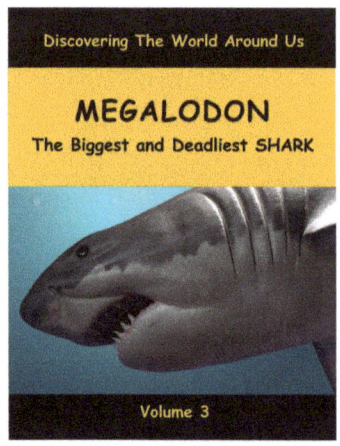

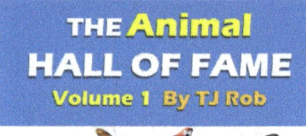

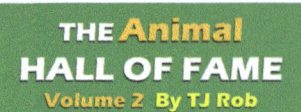

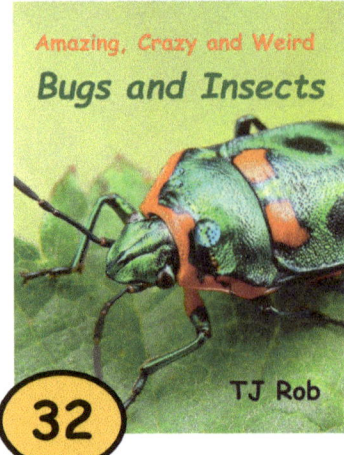
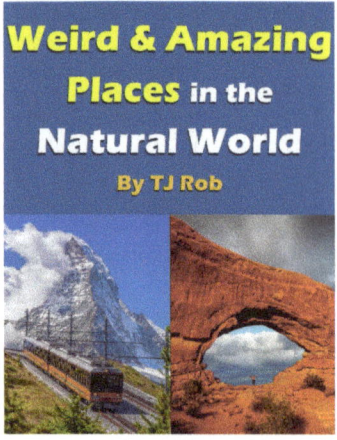

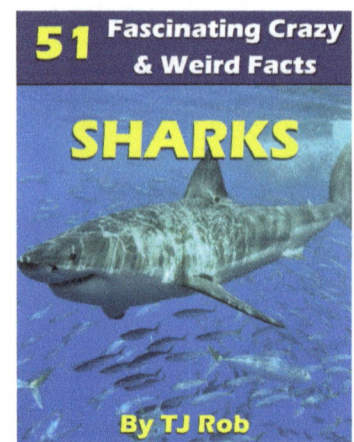

www.ingramcontent.com/pod-product-compliance
Lightning Source LLC
Chambersburg PA
CBHW040006080526
44586CB00027B/2905